The Cemetery in a Garden
150 Years of the
City of London
Cemetery and Crematorium

CITY OF LONDON

By
David Lambert

British Library Cataloguing in Publication Data.
A catalogue record for this book is available from
the British Library

City of London Corporation
City of London Cemetery and Crematorium
Aldersbrook Road
London
E12 5DQ

Copyright © City of London 2006

ISBN 0 85203 087 8
978 0 85203 087 5

Printed and bound by Hobbs the Printers, Totton, Hampshire

Contents

Foreword by The Right Honourable
The Lord Mayor, Alderman David Brewer CMG — Page v

Foreword by Mr John Brewster CC, the Chairman of the
Port Health and Environmental Services Committee of the
City of London Corporation — Page vii

List of Plates — Page ix

1. The landscape before the Cemetery — Page 1

2. The origins of the Cemetery — Page 9

3. 'Planned to perfection': the design of the Cemetery — Page 17

4. 'Completeness and beauty': Haywood's period, 1853-1894 — Page 29

5. 'The Cemetery in a Garden': the Cemetery's development, 1894-1974 — Page 37

6. 'Meeting the needs of the bereaved': the Cemetery in the late twentieth century — Page 47

7. Repair and renewal: the Cemetery in the twenty-first century — Page 53

8. Heritage Trail — Page 57

Foreward by The Right Honourable The Lord Mayor, Alderman David Brewer CMG

The City of London Cemetery is a garden where people are buried. Over the one hundred and fifty years since opening, the City of London Cemetery has developed into England's most impressive cemetery garden landscape and it is rightly recognised as one of the most significant sites of its kind in the world.

This celebratory book takes the reader through the Cemetery's journey from its origins to the present day and describes how it has developed over the years. Walk around the site and you will find an impressive display of the changes in British cemetery culture since the Victorian period: the original Haywood landscape as you enter the impressive entrance; the post-war lawn graves to the rear; London's first municipal crematorium; and the near-by memorial garden - probably the largest of it's kind in the world. The cemetery is an open-air museum displaying our funeral culture and it continues to reflect that culture as it changes today. This historic site still serves a wide and diverse community as the major burial and cremation facility for north-east London, retaining its leading and innovative role in meeting the needs of the bereaved.

In this book you will find the story of an important cultural landscape that has touched upon the lives of millions of people over the last 150 years. This solemn, orderly and beautiful place is a part of our national heritage and I am pleased that, in the cemetery's 150th year, you have the opportunity to find out about the history and future of this great cemetery.

Foreword by Mr John Brewster CC, the Chairman of the Port Health and Environmental Services Committee of the City of London Corporation

When you look around the City of London Cemetery at Aldersbrook, you see the mature vision of our predecessors in the City of London Corporation – a serene and beautiful landscape garden in which the bereaved can find solace. It was a noble vision, to turn away forever from the squalid conditions of the City's crowded churchyards and burial grounds and lay out a truly magnificent modern cemetery on the edge of the metropolis.

The undeniable evidence of the need to close the City's overcrowded burial places was provided by the City's Chief Medical Officer, Dr John Simon. But the vision of the new cemetery belonged to William Haywood, the City's Engineer and Surveyor, who drove through the acquisition of the land and the case for investing in quality in the laying-out of the site, the construction of its buildings and the planting of thousands of trees and shrubs. Haywood employed the nurseryman and gardener William Davidson to oversee the planting but he designed the buildings himself. In addition, for nearly forty years he oversaw its development and expansion. The other individual who needs to be remembered when we look around was the first superintendent, J C Stacey, who retained the position from the Cemetery's opening until 1896.

But this is not a landscape set in aspic. It is a working landscape, which has been adapted over the years in response to the changing needs of the bereaved and of society. Demand for burials grew rapidly after the cemetery opened and from the beginning it provided for all classes of society, not just those who could afford Victorian extravagance. A succession of extensions marked its development throughout the nineteenth century and the first half of the twentieth; extensions into land wisely acquired on Haywood's advice against just such an eventuality. The City of London Corporation was one of the earliest burial authorities to erect a crematorium in response to the Cremation Act of 1902. It was one of the first to lay out an area for lawn burial when that philosophy was introduced after the Second World War. It laid out the stunning Memorial Gardens in the 1960s, and in more recent years has led the way nationally in terms of providing a variety of memorials and burial options, the latest being its new garden for the burial of infants.

But none of these developments would mean very much if they were just history. What makes the Cemetery remarkable today, and this is a sad reflection on the state of cemeteries generally, is its immaculate maintenance. So many cemeteries across the country are in decline, with memorials falling down or being demolished, buildings boarded up, trees ageing and dying. The City of London Corporation has always recognised high standards in the way the cemetery is maintained and the way the bereaved are treated. This takes not just money on the Corporation's part, but dedicated staff who know they are valued for the service they provide.

So I am delighted to celebrate the 150th anniversary of the opening of the Cemetery. This book celebrates its history and the vision of those who created it, but it also celebrates its present as a place for the bereaved, maintained to standards that befit them as well as the City of London Corporation. It also celebrates the prospect of a future of continued excellence to which the City of London Corporation is committed.

John Brewster

Acknowledgements

Many people have studied the history of the Cemetery, and the author gratefuly acknowledges their work. In particular, he would like to thank the following for their help in supplying information during the preparation of this account of the Cemetery: Gary Burks, Sarah Couch, Dr. Doris Francis, Dr. Ian Hussein, Leonie Kallaher, Jeremy Lineham, David McCarthy, David Pescod, Dr. Julie Rugg, Robert Thorne, Jenifer White, John Woodcock and Dr. Roger Watson.

List of Plates

Plate 1   City of London Gates 1913

Plate 2   Interior of Episcopal Chapel - *Main Burial Church*

Plate 3   Interior of Dissenters Chapel - *Reserve Burial Chapel*

Plate 4   View along South Gate Road

Plate 5   Junction of Belfry Road and Anchor Road

Plate 6   Main Burial Church

Plate 7   Burial Chapel (Reserve Chapel)

Plate 8   Cemetery Dray Horses

Plate 9   Staff Outing Early 1900's

Plate 10   Catacomb in winter

Plate 11   City of London Cemetery in the snow

Plate 12   Gardens Way in Memorial Gardens

Plate 13   General Memorial Garden View

Chapter One

The landscape before the Cemetery

Although now presenting a very different appearance from its surroundings, the City of London Cemetery occupies land that was once part of Wanstead Flats. The Flats are part of the southern area of Epping Forest, which extended as far south as Romford Road, the Roman road from London to Colchester. The land was originally part of the manor of Wanstead, and was enclosed around the same time as Wanstead Park, about 1512, at which point Aldersbrook became a separate manor in

Fig 1.
John Nordens Map of Essex 1584

its own right, and the open waste, similar to Wanstead Flats as they now are, was converted to farmland.

Aldersbrook Manor was never on the same scale as the palatial house at Wanstead, but in the sixteenth and seventeenth centuries it was nevertheless a prestigious house and estate, a 'house of name' as recorded on John Norden's map of Essex in 1594 (Fig 1). In the early sixteenth century it was owned and occupied by Sir John Heron, treasurer of the Chamber to Henry VII and Henry VIII, and later by his son, Giles who married the daughter of Sir Thomas More. Later in the century it was occupied by the Earl of Pembroke.

At that time the estate included not only Aldersbrook House, which stood at the eastern end of Aldersbrook Pond, but also a farm house with a pound and outbuildings, built on the north bank of the Pond. Much of the manor was unenclosed waste, and the farm house may well have been built for a warrener to tend the conies or rabbits which the owners of the House enjoyed hunting. The warren remained an important feature of the estate until the early eighteenth century when the land was enclosed for agriculture.

The fortunes of the manor house declined in the seventeenth century. It went through a variety of owners until 1693 when the estate was bought by John Lethieullier, whose son, Smart, succeeded in 1737. The Lethieulliers seem to have been responsible for reviving the manor house and creating a garden and a small park around it and making the old pond into an ornamental lake. Rocque's map of London published in 1750 shows what are probably already mature avenues across the area now occupied by the Cemetery, which in style probably date from John's time, while the gardens east of the pond are attributed to Smart Lethieullier and his wife (Fig 2).

One famous traveller, Bishop Pococke, remarked that Lethieullier had 'made a very pretty improvement there', with 'a beautiful hermitage in a

Fig 2. Rocque's Map of London, 1750

wood, with lawn, water, a mount, parterre etc.' The mount and parterre he attributed to Lethieullier's wife. A detailed survey plan made in 1748 (Fig 3) shows the house with a terrace to the north (looking across what is now the new lawn) and a canal to the south, on the site of the Birches woodland, with further ornamental gardens, including the mount and parterre, enclosed to the south of the canal. Although no images survive, this must have been a sophisticated rococo garden, befitting a gentleman's retreat on the edge of the metropolis.

Smart Lethieullier died in 1760 and the estate passed to his niece and her husband, Sir Edward Hulse. The gardens remained little changed, as

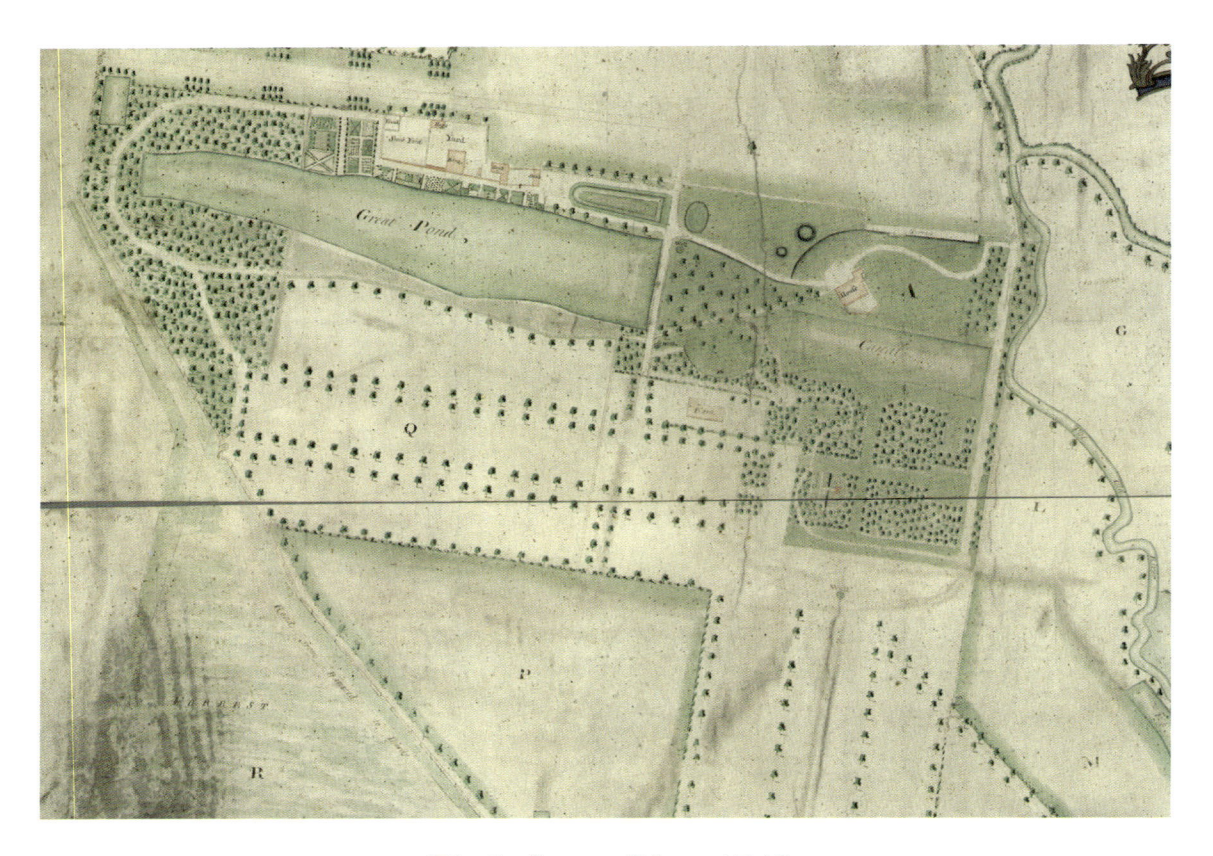

Fig 3. Survey Plan, 1748

recorded on Chapman and Andre's map of Essex in 1777 but in 1786 the estate was sold to Sir James Tylney Long of Wanstead Park. The house was promptly pulled down and its site ploughed over and converted to pasture. The Ordnance Survey of 1799 (Fig 4) records the survival of the great pond, and of at least the site of the canal, but the garden enclosure seems to have succumbed to woodland by this point. The approach from the south was retained as an access road to the farm, while the avenue trees were evidently felled for timber at the same time. The Lethieullier garden was erased forever.

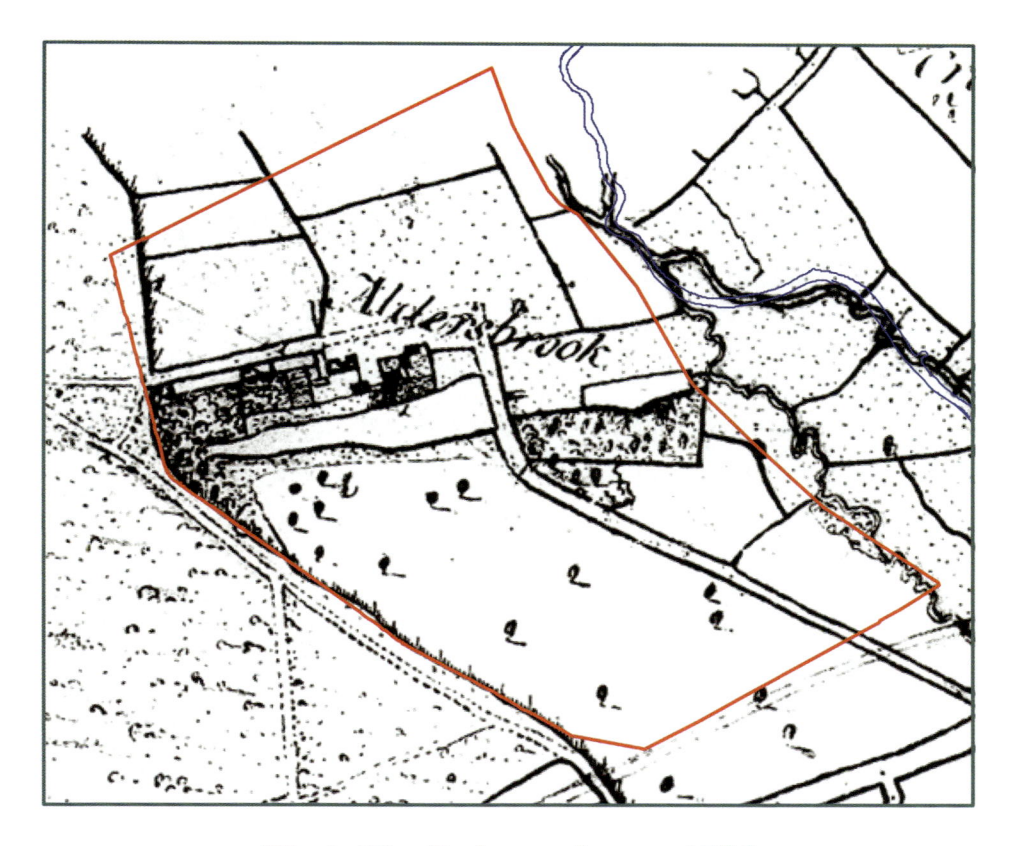

Fig 4. The Ordnance Survey, 1799

Although the Manor House was demolished and its gardens ploughed up, the farmhouse on the north side of the pond however was retained and Aldersbrook remained a prosperous tenant farm up to the time of the Corporation's acquisition.

After the death of Sir James Tylney Long, all the Wanstead estate including Aldersbrook and the site of the Cemetery were inherited by his daughter, Catherine. In 1812 she married William Pole Wellesley who famously squandered the entire fortune by 1824. She died in 1825, but Wellesley later became MP for Essex and Earl of Mornington, and died in 1857. Wellesley was an extremely unpopular local landlord, closing public roads that went through Wanstead Park, enclosing land which had for centuries been treated as common and seeking opportunities for development.

During the Napoleonic Wars, Wanstead Flats were an important military base: in 1806 the King held a review of ten thousand men here, and the Duke of Wellington allegedly was in favour of the Crown obtaining the Flats as an area for military exercises (Fig 5 – An inspection of the West Essex Yeomanry Cavalry on Wanstead Flats, 18 June 1853. The Flats remained an important mustering ground well into the nineteenth century: this event attracted 'immense numbers of spectators from the town').

Throughout the early nineteenth century, pressure grew on the Flats and on Epping Forest in general, from enclosures of the waste by farmers, and from sales by lords of the various manors. Wellesley was the most prominent of local offenders, although in 1817, even the Government considered a bill to allow it to take over 9000 acres of Epping Forest for planting up timber for the Royal Navy. In 1851 the Wellesley family instructed the tenant of Aldersbrook Farm to enclose thirty-four acres of open land along Aldersbrook Road; in the same year Wellesley was in court disputing the enclosure of thirty four acres of the Flats at Cann Hall. Elsewhere in Epping Forest lords of the manors were doing much the same, with a view to potential sale-value.

Pressure was growing from the expanding metropolis. In 1826 a piece of the Aldersbrook estate was sold to build a new prison on, now covered by residential development between Gloucester Road and Colchester Road. In 1838 work began on the new railway from London to Norwich, again taking a slice of the Aldersbrook land.

This then was the situation when the Corporation's surveyor visited the site in 1853 in his exploration of a number of potential sites for a new Cemetery.

Fig 5. An inspection of the West Essex Yeomanry Cavalry on Wanstead Flats, 18 June 1853

Chapter Two

The origins of the Cemetery

By the mid-nineteenth century, the over-crowded state of the churchyards and burial grounds in the City of London had become a serious threat to public health. However, even as early as 1660, the City's churchyards were described as already over-full and were being described as a disgrace and in the wake of the Great Fire, Sir Christopher Wren had already suggested 'cemeteries seated in the outskirts of the town.' Between 1801 and 1851, the population of London rose from 865,000 to 2,362,000. Burial was the only available option for disposal of the dead and the only places available were parish churchyards and dissenters' burial grounds.

During this period, vaults were stacked with coffins, graves were continually being disturbed to make way for new burials and body-snatching became rife. Within the Square Mile and Liberties there were 108 parishes: the burial places were packed with decomposing corpses, often barely covered with earth and it was not uncommon to find them littered with human remains dug up by dogs. In some places re-use of a grave would occur within as little as six months: the ground level of burial grounds rose dramatically in many places to accommodate evermore burials. The stench from these places was horrible, their appearance gruesome and the threat to human health the cause of increasing and more authoritative alarm (Fig. 6 St. Olaves Hart Street).

In 1831, land was acquired at Kensal Green by a new private company for the formation of a commercial Cemetery. Although not opened until 1837, it proved highly popular with the middle classes who could afford

Fig. 6 St. Olaves Hart Street

its fees: by 1840 the value of shares in the General Cemetery Company had more than doubled. By that time the South Metropolitan Cemetery Company had opened Norwood Cemetery (1837), and the London Cemetery Company had opened Highgate (1839) and Nunhead (1840), the same year that the West London and Westminster Company opened Brompton Cemetery. These were all aimed at the middle and upper class markets, but at Abney Park (1840), although again set up and run by a private company, there was a non-conformist determination to serve all classes of society equally. Finally, the Tower Hamlets Cemetery Company opened its new cemetery off the Mile End Road in 1841 to serve the densely populated East End of London.

The City of London could thus be considered slow in responding to the crisis in the City's burial places. Petitions to close churchyards became ever more frequent, and the Corporation's Medical Officer of Health, Dr John Simon, appointed in 1848, was urging the Corporation to close all the City's places of interment. It may be that it was the 1852 Burial Act which forced the Corporation to act, containing as it did a new power to ban burials in parts of the metropolis and making the Commissioners of Sewers a burial authority, with powers to remove bodies from overcrowded City sites for re-interment elsewhere.

The Commissioners of Sewers now began the search for a site for a new cemetery outside the City boundaries, and they ordered their Surveyor, William Haywood, to prepare a report on a suitable site. Haywood (1821-94) was thirty-two: he had trained as an architect and had become Surveyor to the Commissioners in 1845 before being made Surveyor and Engineer in 1853 (Fig. 7). With Sir Joseph Bazalgette he became one of the makers of modern London and worked with him on the Abbey Mills Pumping Station. His greatest work was probably the Holborn Viaduct and its approaches, built from 1866. He was passionately committed to improving the state of public health and took a lifelong interest in the development of the City of London Cemetery.

In the early nineteenth century, cemetery design was concerning not only public health officials and campaigners, but also landscape designers. The great John Claudius Loudon published his book, *On the Laying out of Cemeteries*, in 1843. While primarily concerned with the hygienic disposal of the dead, Loudon also argued that new cemeteries should provide for 'the improvement of the moral sentiment and general taste of all classes, and more especially the great masses of society.' Cemeteries, in contrast to the shocking appearance of many urban churchyards at the time, could and should be beautiful, tranquil places, and he used the term 'garden cemetery' for what he proposed, arguing that it should be 'the sworn foe

Fig. 7 William Haywood

to preternatural fear and superstition.' A cemetery, 'properly designed, laid out, ornamented with tombs, planted with trees, shrubs, and herbaceous plants, all named, and the whole properly kept, might become a school of instruction in architecture, sculpture, landscape-gardening, arboriculture, botany, and in those important parts of general gardening, neatness, order, and high keeping.'

Haywood's report, delivered early in 1853, was scathing on present conditions within the City – he called the churchyards 'over-gorged' and 'disgusting' – and clear on the needs for the future: a site outside the city but easily accessible and on free-draining, agricultural land. The area required was based on average mortality rates for the City, some 3000 a year; on prevailing winds and on the distance for travel, which Haywood envisaged being entirely vehicular.

The Cemetery needed to attract the wealthy as well as to serve the poor. From the start the Commissioners were determined that the new cemetery should be 'a work for posterity as well as the present generation.' The whole spectrum of the City population, rich and poor, Anglican and Dissenters, was to be provided for. For that, and to ensure that it could be used for many generations to come, a high standard of building and planting was required, as well as an area large enough for ground to be reserved for future use.

Haywood's recommendation was for some 200 acres of arable, pasture and meadow land at Aldersbrook, and he submitted a survey drawing of the site to the Commissioners (Fig.8). The site was gently undulating, sloping gradually to the river Roding, and the soil was, in Haywood's enthusiastic words, 'a fine bright gravel, varying in depth from 10 feet to 18 feet.'. It included the farm and the pond, by now half-silted up, a number of mature trees and the rectangular wood containing the old canal and gardens to the south of it. In addition there was a station on the Eastern Counties Railway only a mile away. The purchase was agreed, although not without dispute between the Earl of Mornington and his son over who actually owned the land to sell. However, by the middle of 1854 the purchase was complete and Haywood's masterplan for the new cemetery was ready to be implemented.

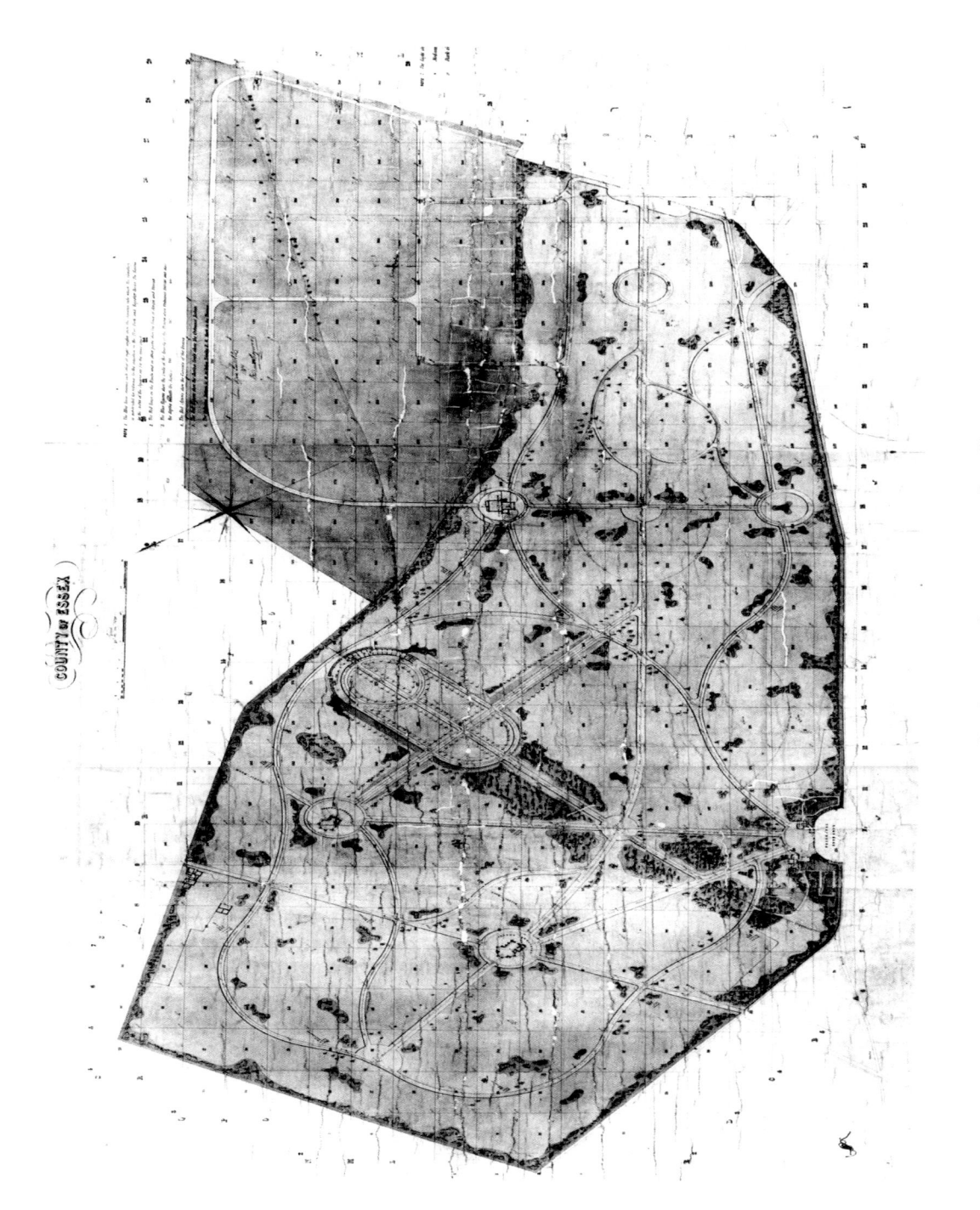

Fig. 8 Haywood's Survey drawing to the Commissioners.

Chapter Three

'Planned to perfection': the design and development of the Cemetery

Haywood's plan for the layout of the Cemetery covered some 90 acres of the 200 purchased, with the rest set aside for future extensions (Fig 9). Work proceeded quickly: between 1854 and 1855 the lake was drained, the buildings demolished and drains and roads laid out. The two chapels were built, one for Anglicans (the Church) (Fig.10)

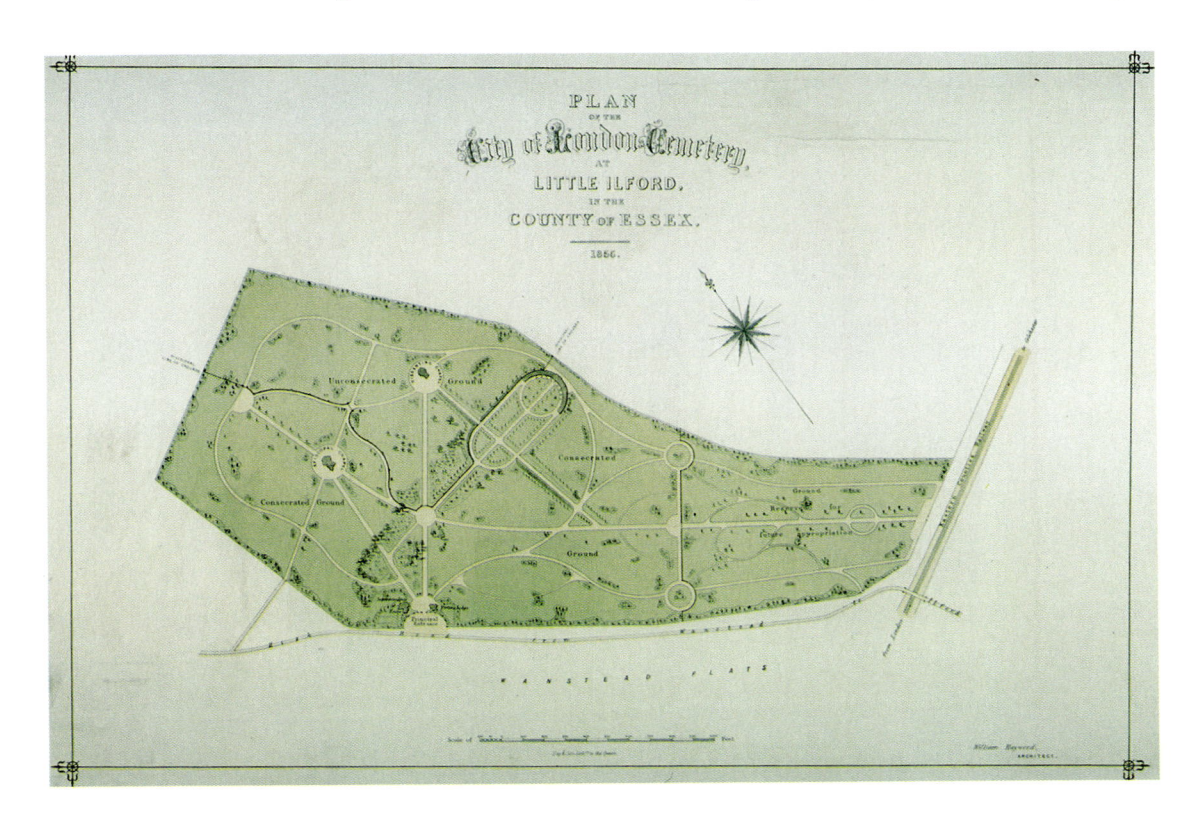

Fig. 9. Haywood's plan for the Cemetery layout, 1856

Fig. 10. The Church

and one for Dissenters (the Chapel) (Fig.11) with consecrated and unconsecrated ground for burials. The Catacombs were built into the eastern end of the former lake and in 1855 and the landscape gardener

Fig. 11. The Chapel

and nurseryman, William Davidson, was commissioned to draw up planting plans with Haywood.

Haywood was responsible for the architectural design of all the buildings built between 1854-55: the main entrance on Aldersbrook Road, the flanking lodge and superintendent's house, the two chapels and the Catacombs. The use of a Gothic revival style contrasted to the neo-classical style used by the earlier cemetery companies at Kensal Green and Highgate.

The entrance has fine metal gates and flanking railings, its grandeur literally announcing arrival in a special place (Fig 12). Over the entrance is a large carved panel with the City of London coat of arms, rather than the religious statue which might have been expected. It was designed to announce entry into a different world, solemn, orderly and beautiful. The contrast between the rough open landscape of the Flats outside the gates

Fig. 12. The Cemetery entrance

and the immaculate layout within remains dramatic, and the designed vistas immediately drew the visitor's eye into the landscape and towards the spiritually uplifting symbolism of the Church and Chapel. The superintendent's house, now the office, is an imposing asymmetric composition. Above the suspended ceiling in the main reception room, its Gothic timber roof still survives. The Porter's Lodge on the opposite side of the gates, now the Haywood Centre, is equally irregular and ornate though appropriately less imposing. From the area immediately inside the gates, shrubberies screened all sight of graves, and colourful flower-beds created a garden-like first impression.

It was a magnificent layout as befitted the size of the site and the ambitions of the Corporation. The layout combines serpentine and straight forms, and the roads were cut to lie below the level of the surrounding ground, 'with a view to their concealment in the landscape.' Given that access is now almost all from the Aldersbrook Road gates, it is important to remember that the layout also reflects the hope that a railway siding would be built directly within the Cemetery at the southern end of Central Avenue; hence the direct route to the Chapel from Central Avenue across the Catacomb valley, and hence the straight lines of South Drive and South Gate Road, which were designed to serve as return routes to the sidings. South Gate was likewise designed principally as an exit. The need for efficient circulation of *cortèges* was recognised from the start and with nearly 10,000 funerals a year at the Cemetery's peak of business in 1871-73, it would have been essential.

The buildings were ingeniously sited so that although both were visible from the entrance gates, once the approach to one or other was taken, the other was no longer visible – hence the slight curve to Central Avenue east of Chapel Avenue, preventing a view of the Church for those heading

Fig. 13. Catacomb Valley

to the Chapel. The Church was designed not only to accommodate the bereaved but as a focal point in the landscape: it is notable that its orientation is not east-west as traditional, but relates to the landscape layout, with its main entrance facing the approach up Church Avenue from the south. Internally there is fine craftsmanship on view, in the woodcarving of bench ends and panels, designed by Haywood, and the unique ironmongery on the doors. The Chapel was designed for non-conformists in a less flamboyant style than the Church with a simpler interior and exterior. It has no steeple, but its main façade again relates to the landscape layout, facing St Andrew's Road and the Holborn monument across Catacomb Valley.

The Catacomb Valley was the last feature to be completed and was the centrepiece of Haywood's design. Nothing like it had been constructed in the other major cemeteries at that time (Fig 13). The lake bed created a natural amphitheatre and the approach, through a shallow valley planted with Rhododendrons and other flowering shrubs, now of course obscured by the modern Crematorium, was equally theatrical (Fig 14). The

Fig 14 Shallow Valley

Catacombs were designed in a more restrained style than the Church and Chapel but overall the composition was pure spectacle, with formal planting of evergreens and broad gravel paths. The catacombs themselves, use of which was falling out of favour by 1856, were never filled, but its importance was as much as a place for promenading as for the disposal of the dead. The design of the Catacombs incorporates steps up to a prospect terrace from which visitors could enjoy views eastward out of the Cemetery over open countryside and Haywood's promotional view showed visitors promenading in a perfect illustration of Loudon's hopes for cemeteries as places of beauty and recreation as well as burial (Fig 15).

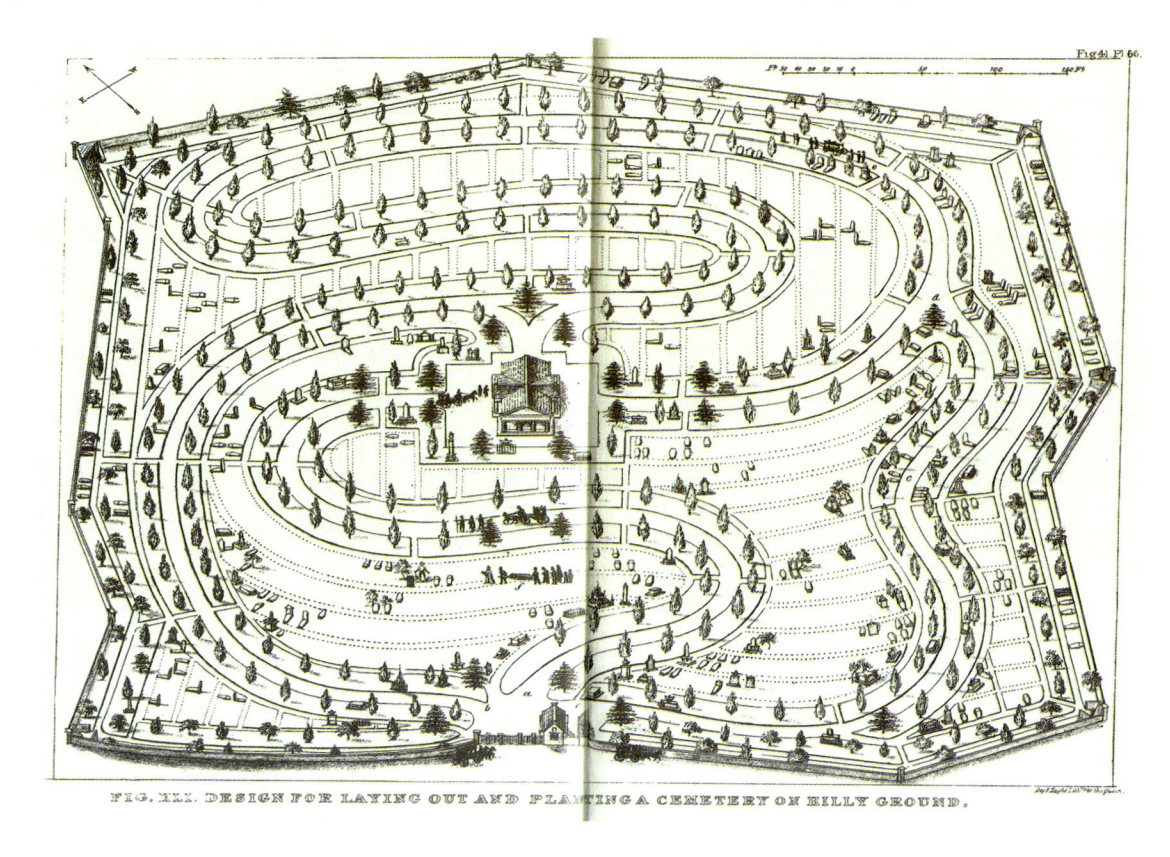

Fig. 15. Loudon's Plan

Fig. 16. Typical shrubberies as planted by Haywood

Consecration was delayed after the Bishop of London, concerned at the loss of income from burials in the City's parish churchyards, insisted that all 106 parishes had to agree to the new Cemetery. Although the Cemetery opened in June 1856, it was not finally consecrated until November of the following year. Forty-nine acres were eventually consecrated, with twenty-one acres left for Dissenters and twenty acres, south-east of St Dionis Road left unappropriated. Iron posts marked the division between consecrated and unconsecrated ground: part of that boundary is recorded in the line and name of Divisional Road.

The site had a number of mature trees already existing, chiefly around the north and west of the silted-up pond. Haywood's scheme involved the planting of many more trees, notably in a perimeter belt around the entire boundary except for the railway boundary where, presumably, he still hoped to establish a siding. He also planted a large number of trees and shrubs in scattered clumps and shrubberies (Fig 16). These clumps were planted strategically at junctions and along the roads and paths to direct the eye and give variety to the views. Haywood's initial scheme did not include the regular road-side trees which are now so characteristic, but tree-planting went on throughout the nineteenth century and these were mostly added around the end of the century.

By 1863 the planting had been much augmented, principally with ornamental conifers which, being evergreen, were considered suitable for cemeteries. However, these were in the minority and the absence of the heavy gloom created by a predominance of conifers was and remains one of the Cemetery's notable characteristics: one description from 1929 stated 'Here are no trees of mourning – cypress nor yew nor weeping willow; only seemly beauty as of some great park adorned'. The Cemetery's tree-stock still has a high percentage of deciduous forest trees – Plane, Beech, Oak, Lime, Horse Chestnut – and this creates its distinctive character (Fig 17).

The shrubbery clumps were probably dominated by Rhododendron from the start but included a wide range of other shrubs and flowering trees: Lilac, Holly, Laurustinus, Acuba, Forthsythia, Olearia, Skimmia, Larch, Privet, Azalea and Laburnum, Crataegomespilus, Hawthorn, Ailanthus, Arbutus, Magnolia and Caucasian Wing-Nut were all well-established by the early twentieth-century.

William Davidson oversaw the planting of the Cemetery for Haywood. Davidson was a well-known figure, former head gardener at Shrubland Park in Suffolk, one of the most elaborate of Victorian gardens, and an

Fig. 17. Cemetery Trees

authority on ornamental planting. He would also have ensured that annual bedding displays were of the highest quality all year round: a description of the planting in front of the superintendent's house, now the office, refers to 'an expanse of green lawn, flower beds and borders, with geraniums red and pink, heliotrope, begonias, pentstemons, yellow violas, creamy hydrangeas, thickets of rhododendrons and laurels.'

    Haywood planned for burials in three categories, first, second and third-class. The areas along the drives were reserved for first-class burials, for which a substantial memorial stone was required; the rows behind were for second-class with third-class behind that. Within those zones, the bereaved could choose a site anywhere in the Cemetery. He also indicated that certain areas were not to be used for burials, in particular the Catacomb Valley and the land immediately inside the entrance gates.

The Corporation had a duty to bury paupers without charge, and it was the areas away from the main drives and on the perimeter of the Cemetery which were used for common graves. Haywood was keen to avoid 'the broad distinction between rich and poor' which would result from allocating specific areas for common graves, and so dispersed them across the entire Cemetery. These were marked by small, simple stones, thousands of which have been cleared away during the twentieth century (Fig 18). A group has been preserved in the north of the Cemetery between Anchor Road and North Boundary Road.

Fig 18 Common Graves

Chapter Four

'Completeness and beauty': Haywood's period, 1853-1894

William Haywood maintained his interest in the Cemetery until his death in 1894, overseeing all significant changes and preparing many drawings himself. He chose to be cremated (in itself a progressive decision at the time) at the Cremation Society's new crematorium at Woking, and his ashes were entombed in the

Fig 19 Haywood's Memorial

Gothic memorial on Church Avenue which he designed himself (Fig 19). However, equally important to the development of the Cemetery was the presence of John Chapple Stacey, the superintendent who remained in post between 1856 and 1896 (Fig 20). It was Stacey who made all day-to-day decisions, approving individual monuments, planning the location of

Fig 20 Stacey's Memorial

burials and the expansion of the Cemetery, as well as supervising the landscape's planting and maintenance. He is commemorated not only by a plaque in the Church but also by the name of the circular junction and bed at the southern end of St Dionis Road, Stacey's Circle.

Not surprisingly, the Cemetery proved successful with burials rising from 280 in 1856 to 8,104 in 1861, and maintaining a level of around 6000 per annum throughout the nineteenth century. Haywood wrote in one of his reports, 'There is no instance upon record of a place of sepulture, which has been so much used in so short a space of time.' The reserved ground south of St Dionis Road was rapidly incorporated, and the first extension into the unused land owned by the Corporation was of fourteen acres in 1861, with another of some twenty-five acres in 1874.

One of the notable elements in the landscape we see today is the collection of monuments to the reinterred dead of a number of City parishes. In 1866, the construction of the Holborn Viaduct necessitated the clearance of the churchyards of St Andrew's and St Sepulchre's Holborn. Between eleven and twelve thousand bodies were removed from the former alone, and reinterred at the City of London Cemetery. A few years later as a result of the Union of Benefices Act 1860, a number of City parishes were amalgamated, resulting in a number of churches becoming redundant and subsequently demolished during the 1870s. Development on former burial grounds continued into the 1890s and the dead of several more churchyards were removed to the City of London.

In total, remains from 38 City churchyards were reinterred here, some of which were marked by substantial monuments, mainly on Central Avenue. The most imposing is that to St Andrew's and St Sepulchre's Holborn (Fig 21), but All Hallows Bread Street has a massive Gothic monument while St Martin Outwich's is an eccentric essay in high Gothic;

Fig. 21. St Andrew's & St Sepulchre's

St Alphege was paved with headstones moved from the churchyard, with many beautiful examples of stone-cut script. The remains of the great seventeenth-century scientist, astronomer, engineer and architect Robert Hooke are buried with those of others re-interred from St Helen's Bishopsgate, and commemorated by a fine monument on Central Avenue. It is notable that the monument to St Andrew's and St Sepulchre's was precisely located to act as a focal point, or eyecatcher in the landscape, in the view along St Andrew's Road from the Chapel.

In addition, the Cemetery accommodated re-interments from City plague pits; from the Royal Orphanage at Wanstead, and from the burial grounds at the Hospital for Poor French Protestants, Bath Street, Christ's Hospital, Newgate Street and Newgate Prison itself.

Compared to some of the private cemeteries such as Highgate or Norwood, City of London has relatively few major family monuments. Pauper burials accounted for almost 90% of the burials in the nineteenth century: in 1905, fifty-three years after the Cemetery had opened, there had been 31,393 private interments but 274,065 common interments. A few of the tiny headstones that marked common graves have been retained, although most have long since been cleared away. It has been said that the City of London's grandeur lies in the serried ranks of relatively modest memorials rather than in individual set pieces. However, those that line Church Avenue form, as a group, one of the great Cemetery landscapes in the country.

Tree-planting in the Cemetery continued seemingly year-on-year. By 1863 a significant number of conifers had been introduced, notably Cedars, although Irish Yew and Holm Oak were also favoured. The evergreens originally planted in the Catacomb Valley were replaced with Horse Chestnuts c1870-80s. The planting of avenue trees along the main routes seems to have begun around the same time, judging by the age of the trees, but they are not uniform. Horse Chestnut, Lime, London Plane and even Cherry were all used in different stretches, creating a pleasant variety in the character of the roads.

During the nineteenth century, the Cemetery flourished with a number of extensions into the reserved land and improvements to the facilities, such as heating and the addition of a lady's waiting room at the lodge, a bathroom for the superintedent's house, and tree-planting on areas of common graves which had been filled up. Before 1863 a gardener's cottage was built on the north side of the Cemetery, with a stable and a coach house to the rear. A large walled garden was used as a nursery, and extensive greenhouses were built in 1913.

Until 1897 the old public footpaths still crossed the Cemetery, one going straight across from Belfry Road on the west past the Chapel. For security reasons, Haywood had been anxious to close them from at least 1875, but it took some time before agreement over a diversion was reached. A short section survives in the straight path between the circle around the Church and Divisional Road.

Outside the Cemetery, the continuing erosion of Wanstead and Epping's open land had continued. In 1851 Hainault Forest had been disafforested and enclosed, which led inexorably to its development. In 1871, a rally to protest against the enclosures and to 'Save the Forest' attracted thousands from across east London. The City's purchase of Aldersbrook for the Cemetery encouraged it to become involved as a neighbouring land-owner with rights of pasturage, and it took a lead in the defence of common rights throughout the Forest. In 1876 it bought Cann Hall waste and subsequently, in 19 different parcels, purchased the rest of the Forest. In 1878 the Epping Forest Act was passed, appointing the Corporation as the Conservators of the Forest and ensuring the preservation of the Forest as open land for public enjoyment. Thus, although now so different from the rough open land of the Forest and the neighbouring Wanstead Flats, in fact the Cemetery and the landscape outside its gates are intimately linked in history (Fig 22).

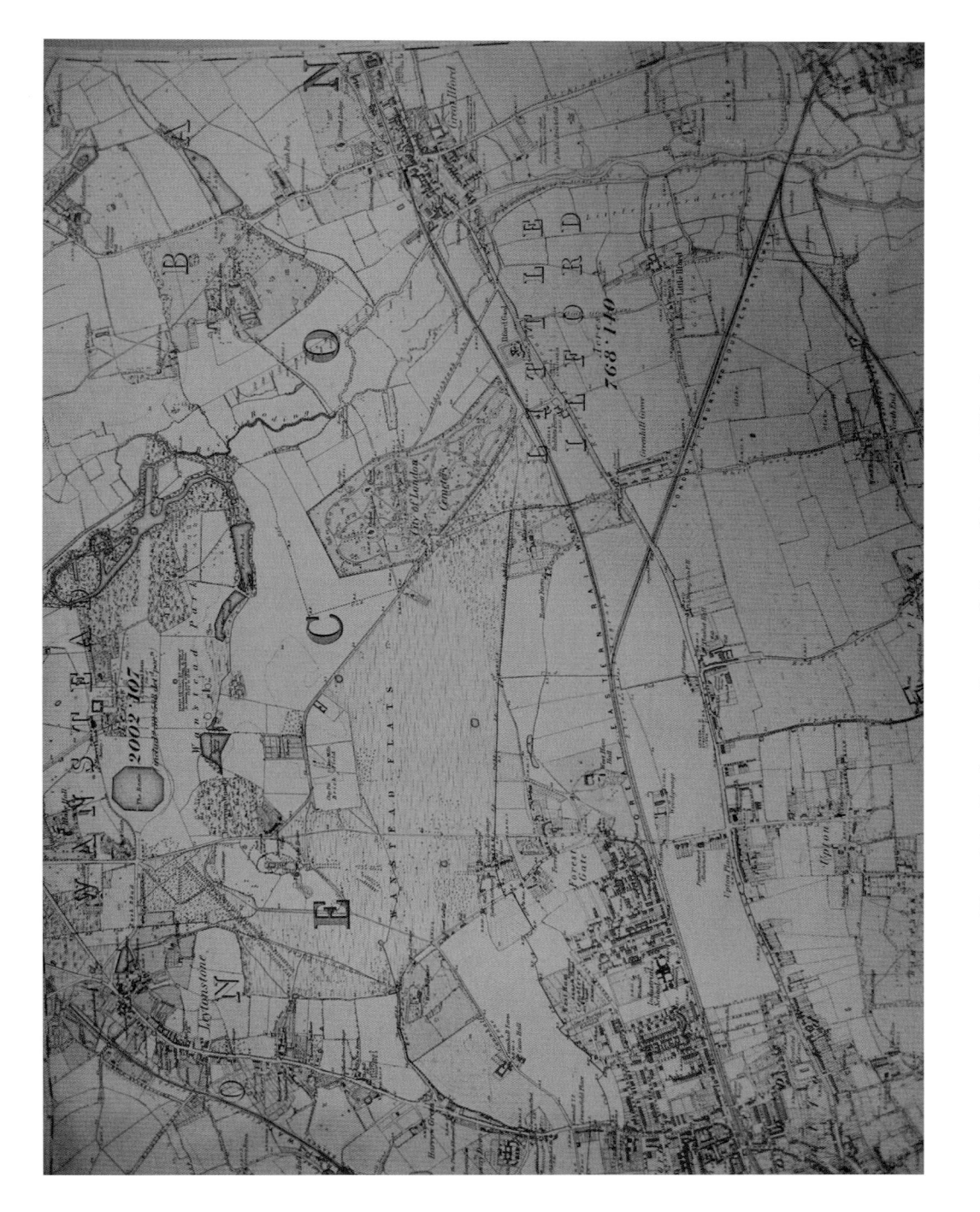

Fig. 22. Ordnance Survey Map of Little Ilford, 1877

Chapter Five

'The Cemetery in a Garden': the Cemetery's development, 1894-1974

Haywood died in 1894 and Stacey retired two years later. By that time the Cemetery was thriving. A promotional booklet produced by the Corporation in 1929, called *The Cemetery in a Garden*, records in words and photographs the Cemetery in its prime. It is very clear that the Cemetery was regarded by the Corporation as much more than just a burial and cremation facility: that it was a public garden, 'where none need be compelled to the thought of death, but where all can forget the world awhile.'

However, just like the churchyards before them, the new cemeteries around London came under increasing pressure as they filled up. Unlike other countries, Britain's legislation made no provision for re-using graves: disturbing human remains, even if completely decomposed, was and is illegal. As a result, there was a logistical timetomb ticking in all the new cemeteries, even in one so well provided for and spacious as the City of London.

One solution which came to be proposed in the second half of the nineteenth century was cremation. A Cremation Society was formed in London in 1874, to promote the idea, at first viewed as eccentric and unnatural. Parliament was unwilling to consider it, so the Society erected a crematorium on land at Woking bought from the London Necropolis Company which ran Brookwood Cemetery there. After the attempted prosecution in 1884 of Dr. William Price for cremating his infant child, named Jesus Christ and born to him at the age of eighty-three, on a hilltop near Llantrissant, it was ruled that cremation was not an offence provided it caused no offence to others, and in 1885 the first cremation took place at Woking. Gradually, more crematoria were built although it was not until the Cremation Act of 1902 that it was formally recognised.

Promptly, the Commissioners decided to construct a Crematorium at the City of London Cemetery. This was to be London's first municipal crematorium which opened in 1904. It was designed by the City Architect, D J Ross, in a version of Haywood's Gothic style. Its siting on one of the two circles on St Dionis Road, meant it sat well in the Haywood landscape, helped by generous planting immediately around it (Fig 23).

Fig. 23 London's first municipal crematorium, 1904

The public was still wary of cremation and take-up was slow. In 1909 the number of urn burials was a mere thirty-one. To promote the Crematorium, the Corporation began to develop the Memorial Gardens, initially as a small area near the Crematorium. In 1928 the Superintendent proposed an elaborate rockery on the north-west side of Limes Avenue with a Garden of Rest to the south-east, immediately behind the Crematorium. A more ambitious scheme soon followed, to adapt part of the Catacombs as a columbarium for the storage of urns, with a Garden of Remembrance in front. In the event neither of the schemes was taken forward, although niches for urns were constructed in the Catacombs and a sunken garden on one side of Limes Avenue with a pond on the other were built and remain today (Fig 24).

Fig. 24 The Sunken Garden from 1950

In 1949, Corporation policy changed drastically, with the adoption of the new practice of lawn burial, that is, serried ranks of uniform headstones without kerbs around the grave. Lawn burial was cheap and reduced the Corporation's burden of maintaining untended but elaborate headstones. It was also, more positively, inspired by the work of the Imperial War Graves Commission, which had already laid out a small enclosure on St Dionis Road, just north-east of Stacey's Circle, after the First World War, incorporating the Sword of Sacrifice monument designed by Sir Reginald Blomfield (Fig 25) and a second after the Second World War. The style suited the new mood of social equality engendered by the post-

Fig. 25 Memorial - First World War

war Labour Government. Brenda Colvin, one of the great landscape architects of the post-war period, wrote of the old Victorian style of memorialisation: 'the worse effects are produced by the cult of individuality run wild; unbridled, irresponsible individuality, especially manifested in the memorials and headstones, whose lack of orderly, unifying design makes eyesores of many urban cemeteries.' Lawn burial was seen as a positive advance, representing the same kind of equality in death that the War Graves Commission upheld.

The first lawn graves (now known as the Old Lawn) were laid out on land previously kept in reserve. Six acres were brought into the Cemetery in 1950, four of which were dedicated to new private graves, and two to common graves. This had until now been used for pasture and later for allotments. As with cremation, take-up was initially slow, but gradually, people warmed to the lawn graves, with their restrained, regular planting, and low cost. Choice was limited: the area was laid out in a grid pattern within a frame of beech and holly hedges, with planting between the rows of headstones, the height and design of which were restricted. The area still illustrates the austere, calm beauty which was the policy's ideal (Fig 26). It is thus mistaken to think that, as one modern critic put it, Haywood 'would surely have condemned the monotonous lawn cemetery policy adopted since 1951 for coffin burial, which ignores any pretence at landscaping.' On the contrary, the lawn graves were laid out on a highly conscious aesthetic principle, albeit one which has since become blurred by more individual planting and materials.

Further increases to the Cemetery to accommodate more lawn graves followed. In 1959 the Corporation took into the Cemetery the land on which the new lawns are now laid out, to the north-east of the original Cemetery, which had been used in the interim as a sports ground for

Fig. 26 Lawn Style Graves

tennis and cricket (Fig 27). Not all new graves were so restrained: the most flamboyant of individual private monuments is the Vigiland memorial located just off Chapel Avenue and erected in 1955 (Fig 28).

In 1953, the Corporation decided to revive the idea of Memorial Gardens and commissioned a plan from the landscape architect Richard Sudell for a large area formerly used for common graves. Sudell had been a founder and first chairman of the British Association of Garden Architects, which later became the Institute of Landscape Architects: he was a great promoter of small, domestic gardens and his design reflects much of the post-war, Festival of Britain spirit. He used modern materials

Fig. 27 Lawn Style Graves circa 1959

such as coloured concrete, extensive paving, and his design was based on intimate enclosures of different characters, bright colours, crisp geometrical forms, and an economical choice of standard roses, small flowering trees and other plants (Fig 29).

Sudell termed his design a Memorial *Garden* and there was clearly an overall design despite the sub-divisions: the enclosures took their characters

Fig. 28. Vigiland Memorial

from the predominance of a particular flower with dedicated beds of carnations, delphiniums, irises, azaleas, lilies, and of course, roses. He included a sunken garden with two lily ponds, which were not built, and an Erica or heather garden, which was. Although he retained one or two of the best Victorian specimen trees, such as the Beech and the London Plane, the contrast with the park-like grandeur of Haywood's design could hardly be greater. Sudell's gardens would have reminded visitors of their own domestic gardens, or inspired them to emulation. They formed a landscape in which people felt at home rather than over-awed.

Sudell's plan occupied only part of the present Memorial Gardens and the first extension north of Gardens Way to Limes Avenue was laid out c. 1962-64, with a further extension across Willow Road in the early 1970s.

During the Second World War a corrugated iron mortuary was erected just beyond the Catacombs terrace, although it was never in fact used for

Fig. 29 Memorial Gardens Dedications

that purpose. In turn, this seems to have heralded the use of the land beyond that as a dump, which has gradually grown to occupy over two acres of the Cemetery, being used now for recycling of all the green waste from the site.

Chapter Six

'Meeting the needs of the bereaved': the Cemetery in the late twentieth century

After the Second World War, cremation became significantly more popular. Demand rose throughout the fifties and sixties, outstripping the capacity of the old Crematorium despite extensions and improvements, the last in 1961. By 1968, work had begun on designing a new Crematorium, which opened in 1974 with the hope that it would meet demand for the next forty years.

Designed by the Corporation's architect's department, under the direction of Edwin Chandler, it was sited just to one side of Rhododendron Avenue in the angle of Chapel Avenue and Central Avenue. Its style is strikingly modern and reflects the new secular spirit of the times (Fig 30). Although the location was evidently intended to preserve the vista to the Catacombs, in practice its porch and arrivals area effectively blocked that view. In addition, the spacious circle at the junction of Central Avenue and Chapel Avenue was turned into an irregular and tight meeting of roads, while the view into the Cemetery from the Catacombs viewing terrace is now dominated by the Crematorium's form. Although the setting of the building was originally bounded by St Andrew's Road, a substantial area to the east was later paved and fenced for floral tributes, eating further into the setting of the Catacombs.

By the 1970s, the Cemetery had incorporated all available land from the original Corporation holding. Lawn graves were expanding rapidly and cremation was becoming the preferred method of disposal. The Cemetery and Crematorium had become the major provider not only for

Fig. 30 Modern Crematorium

the City but also for this area of north-east London. Because of its size and the resources of the Corporation, it remained viable while many other London cemeteries had filled up and were facing a spiral of decline as revenue from burial charges to pay for maintenance dwindled.

The design and materials of headstones in the lawn graves have been allowed to become much more varied, and although the absence of kerbs was intended to make mowing easier, in practice the area in front of many headstones has been taken over for little gardens or temporary memorials such as wind-chimes. The regular planting between the stones has often been replaced with shrubs chosen and planted by grave-owners.

A large number of fast-growing evergreen hedges were planted in the 1970s and 80s, not only in the extensions to the Memorial Gardens but also in the Haywood landscape, notably to screen the site of the old graves from those visiting the modern Crematorium. The extension of the Memorial Gardens included the construction of garden enclosures bounded by walls made from thousands of cleared kerb-stones. A paved area for floral tributes built to the west of the old Crematorium by 1960 was extended in this period together with a large car park.

The Cemetery's range of glasshouses, erected in 1913, was pulled down in 1992. Cemetery-workers housing was constructed immediately north of the old Gardener's Cottage between 1960 and 1975. New offices and workshops were constructed to the north of the old Superintendent's House around the same time, and the Cemetery's dump, known as the Shoot, has spread over a greater and greater area.

The setting of the Cemetery had changed enormously in the twentieth century. The Edwardian terraces and villas of the Aldersbrook estate were built from 1899 onwards on land sold by the Earl of Mornington. Developers were attracted by the proximity of Manor Park station, opened in 1872 and rebuilt in 1893-4. In 1899 East Ham Urban District Council built the new isolation hospital and in 1910, West Ham Board of Guardians built the Aldersbrook Children's Homes. An elementary school was added in 1907 and an infants school in 1911. The parade of shops on Aldersbrook Road was built to serve the new estate in 1904. Although Forest Drive retains a unique character as it passes over the railway bridge out of Manor Park and into the landscape of the Flats, by the end of the century Aldersbrook Road was a busy thoroughfare, with a roundabout immediately outside the Cemetery gates, making the Cemetery within seem more of an oasis than ever. At the same time, for all the contrast it presents with Wanstead Flats outside the gates, it is part of an ecological continuum with the open space outside, forming with Epping Forest, Wanstead Flats and Wanstead Park, a substantial part of a wonderfully diverse range of habitats, stretching across this part of east London.

Unlike many cemeteries, the City of London has continued to serve the needs of the bereaved of east London.

At the turn of the twenty-first century the Cemetery was a landscape of superb beauty, immaculately maintained, with a wealth of architectural and horticultural treasures. Its trees represented not only the mature planting of the Victorians, but a continued tradition of prize specimens planted throughout the twentieth century, not only in the Haywood landscape but also in the lawns and the Memorial Gardens. One or two trees survive from the pre-Cemetery landscape, including the magnificent Beech and Oak at the end of Forges Road, an equally grand Oak at the north-eastern end of Belfry Road, and the Horse Chestnut near New Road just north of the junction with Poplar Road, close to the site of the original Aldersbrook Manor. In the Birches woodland there are some large Oaks and Horse Chestnuts which again pre-date the Cemetery and even some Yews which must be the descendants of the rococo garden planting of Smart Lethieullier and his wife.

From the nineteenth century there are the noble London Planes around the junction leading to the modern Crematorium, the English and Irish Yew, Deodar and Lebanon Cedars that dot the landscape, Yew, Scots Pine and Holm Oak in the perimeter belt, as well as a notable weeping Ash, Strawberry Tree, Turkey Oak and Weeping Silver Lime, Monkey Puzzle and Chinese Ash. The Horse Chestnut, Lime and London Plane planted to line the roads probably date from the late nineteenth century and early twentieth century. Twentieth-century specimen trees include Tree of Heaven, Fern-leaved Beech, Copper Beech, Caucasian Wing-Nut, Gingko, the Indian Bean Tree, a glorious range of Japanese Maples, and such exotics as the two Brewers Weeping Spruce planted as part of the now grassed-over garden of the Stepney Civilian War Memorial. The Memorial Gardens have a wide range of smaller flowering trees, such as the Snowy Meipilus, the Golden Rain Tree, Maples and Cherries. The Corporation has produced a full-colour Tree Trail to the Cemetery brochure available from the administration office.

Chapter Seven

Repair and renewal:
the Cemetery in the twenty-first century

By the beginning of the new millennium, it was clear that the Cemetery was under an unsustainable pressure to find burial space, and to accommodate an ever-wider range of requirements and demands from the bereaved. City of London Cemetery is widely regarded as one of the very best cemeteries in the country, with immaculate levels of maintenance, staffing and service, reflected in its holding a Green Flag and a Green Heritage award. In 2001 and 2004 it won the prestigious Cemetery of the Year award and it is frequently held up as an example to others.

The adoption of the Charter for the Bereaved in 2000 put the onus on the Corporation to meet the needs of the bereaved, a subtle but profound change from the days of Haywood and Stacey when the bereaved had to fit their demands into the Corporation's own strictures and regulations.

The Corporation has responded positively to this challenge, providing a wide range of options and services. It has dedicated an area for woodland burial; it has provided two types of standardised headstone, the Classic graves, built in reconstituted stone for the burial of both coffins and caskets; it has constructed concrete vaults in a gravelled area, known as the Willows; and most recently it has created an enclosure for baby graves. A monument to Lord Shiva has recently been erected by the Hindu community, while the needs of a multicultural society are reflected in the forms of and inscriptions on different graves. In addition, the refurbishment of the old lodge in 2003 has provided a florist shop and a café overlooking the old lodge garden – both proving to be instant successes. This is a modern and thriving Cemetery.

But responding to an ever-wider range of new demands sometimes makes it difficult to keep in view the over-arching need to conserve what makes the Cemetery such a special place. Burial space is limited and in some areas, new graves have been squeezed into verges which had long been left open and spacious. The lawn graves are subject to pressure from visitors, some demanding greater diversity, some greater restriction. Demand for access has resulted in a number of new, straight paths being constructed in and around the Haywood landscape. There is enormous pressure to accommodate car-travel for visitors but at the same time pressure to check speeds and reduce traffic to make the place safe and preserve its tranquillity. And like all burial authorities, the Corporation faces the immense responsibility of making sure all monuments are safe for the general public, a responsibility which many other authorities meet simply by taking them down.

In addition, the wildlife value of the site has come to be recognised as part of a green network across the whole of east London, and across Epping Forest and Wanstead Flats in particular. The site of the eighteenth-century canal and gardens of Aldersbrook Manor is now a substantial and ecologically important woodland, known as 'The Birches', while the wide variety of well-maintained trees and shrubs make the Cemetery a haven for wildlife. At the same time, the site's educational value as a place for schoolchildren to visit and learn about history, wildlife and architecture, and its amenity value as a place to visit for a quiet walk or even a cycle ride, are being increasingly recognised – all of which need to be assessed against the need to preserve the Cemetery as a place serving the needs of the bereaved.

With all these conflicting pressures, the Corporation decided in 2002 that there was a risk of allowing the special character of the Cemetery to be gradually and inadvertently eroded. It commissioned a Conservation Management Plan, jointly funded by the Corporation and the Heritage Lottery Fund, to look at the site's history and development over the last hundred and fifty years, and to set down policies for future management.

The Plan was completed in 2004, and already a number of initiatives have been set up. An area of the Haywood landscape has been designated the Conservation Lawn section, for graves with restrictions on materials and designs, in order that they fit better into the predominant character. Wildlife areas of less visited older graves have been designated, in which grass is allowed to grow long to encourage wildlife and wild flowers. A wildlife trail through the Birches woodland has been established. And perhaps most significantly, a panel has been set up to assess all the older memorials in terms of their historic and ecological interest with a view to deciding whether they should be repaired, re-used or demolished. A rolling programme of monument repair by the Cemetery's conservation management team has been established. The Corporation is experimenting with traffic restrictions and has introduced a free bus-service around the Cemetery. On the landscape, many of the evergreen hedges planted in the Haywood landscape have been removed and the overgrown shrubberies cut back to allow replanting.

The key to the future sustainability of the Cemetery though lies in unlocking the potential for future burials. The Government is currently considering the arguments for allowing graves to be re-used after a set period of around seventy-five years, rather than left undisturbed in perpetuity. Because of its excellent records, the Corporation is already able to identify unused space in graves, which were often dug to accommodate up to six burials, space not always used by a particular family. But filling unused grave space will not in itself allow the Corporation to meet ongoing demand. The ability to re-use graves, after a set period, using the method known as lift-and-deepen, whereby a grave is excavated and in the event of finding any remains they are reinterred to a greater depth in the same grave, would allow the Cemetery to continue to serve for many decades to come, while still preserving its unique character. But this depends on new legislation and at the time of writing the Government has still to make up its mind on the matter.

Chapter Eight

Heritage Trail

In the one hundred and fifty years that the City of London Cemetery and Crematorium has been in operation there have been many people of note either buried or cremated here. These range from sporting personalities, entertainment personalities, criminals and their victims, to heroes in the truest sense of the word and local people whose lives have formed part of our heritage.

The City of London Cemetery & Crematorium runs regular Heritage Tours on which the story of the cemetery and those at rest here are told. There is also a Heritage Brochure to complement these tours.

Some of those on these tours are:-

Sporting personalities.

There are two sportsmen of note buried within our grounds and they are John Roberts the man who popularised billiards, and in more recent years the great footballer Bobby Moore.

Though John Roberts was buried in the City of London Cemetery in 1893, his grave was never marked by a headstone. It was fortunate that in 1988 a group of billiard devotees got together and were able to raise enough money to have a headstone erected to his memory. Roberts is credited with the promotion of billiards not only in this country but around the world and is recognised, as stated on his headstone, as the Father of Modern Billiards.

Our second sportsman of note is Bobby Moore. Bobby Moore is one of the most popular of football stars and first came to prominence in 1958 when he made his début for West Ham's first team. Over the next few years Bobby's career went from strength to strength until he was appointed captain of the England team for the first time on 20th May 1962. The following year he was named as Footballer of the year. The event Bobby will always be remembered for is the World Cup final in 1966, when he led the England team to victory over West Germany.

Moore sadly passed away on 24th February 1993 after losing his battle against cancer. His cremated remains are now buried in our memorial gardens and are one of the most visited sites in the cemetery.

Law and Order

The Whitechapel Murders
There are many cases of murder that have caught the public imagination over the years but none as lasting as that of the Whitechapel Murders and the name of the person known around the world as Jack the Ripper.

The reign of terror that surrounded the infamous murders surprisingly only lasted for a very short period of time. The first murder took place on Friday 31st August 1888 and the last just ten weeks later on Friday 9th November 1888, but during that period five women lost their lives and a legend was born.

Of the five victims two are buried in the City of London Cemetery. The first, Mary Ann (Polly) Nichols, and the fourth victim, Catherine Eddowes, were both buried in unmarked public graves. In response to many visitors asking to see the location of the burial places of these unfortunate women the graves have been marked by special plaques. These plaques have been featured in documentaries and pictures of them are also on the Jack the Ripper website.

Thompson/Bywaters Murder Case

A local murder case dating back to the 1920s that still stirs interest is that of the Thompson/Bywaters murder case. The details of the case are simple enough. A young married woman, Edith Thompson started an affair with a young man, Freddie Bywaters. The result of the affair was that Edith's husband Percy Thompson was attacked and stabbed to death by Freddie on the night of 4th October 1922.

At the subsequent trial, many of the intimate letters written to Freddie Bywaters by Edith were entered into evidence and the contents were damming. There were descriptions of how Edith was trying to get rid of Percy by poisoning him, and letters goading Freddie to take action to rid them of Percy.

The result of the trial was that Freddie and Edith were found guilty of the murder of Percy Thompson and both were hanged at 9am on January 1923.

Since the trial there have been attempts to get Edith pardoned for her part in the murder of Percy Thompson. Several books on the case have been published and in 2001 a feature film was made entitled *Another Life*. The murder of Percy Thompson is controversial to this day and it is the body of the luckless Percy that is buried in the City of London Cemetery.

The Houndsditch Murders

On the night of 16th December 1910, police were called to a disturbance in Houndsditch. The disturbance was caused by an attempted break-in to a jeweller's shop in Houndsditch and resulted in the deaths of three City of London policemen and the serious wounding of two others by a gang of Latvian anarchists.

The funeral service for the three dead policemen, Sergeants Bentley (Fig. 31) and Tucker (Fig. 32) and Constable Choat, took place in St Paul's Cathedral with the subsequent burial of both Bentley and Tucker at the City of London Cemetery. The three murdered officers, along with the wounded Sergeant Bryant and Constable Woodhams, were all awarded the Kings Police Medal.

Fig 31. Sergeant Bentley.
Courtesy of the City of London Police Museum

The murders of the unarmed policemen caused outrage throughout Britain and over the following couple of weeks several of the gang were captured by the London police.

On New Year's Day 1911 the last two members of the gang were found to be in hiding at 100 Sidney Street. On the morning of 3rd January the famous Siege took place with two hundred men used to cordon off the block. Unbelievably, the two men inside the house had superior weaponry and a seemingly unlimited supply of ammunition and a call went out for troops from the Tower of London to be used to break the siege.

The Home Secretary of the time, Winston Churchill gave permission to use whatever force was necessary and then rushed down to Sidney Street to see what was happening.

After several grandiose ideas of how to break the siege failed, it finally came to an end when a fire started inside the house. As the house became a blazing inferno those outside trained their guns on the doors fully expecting the anarchists to come out and surrender. This never happened and the last two members of the gang died in the house. The two anarchists as well as the two murdered police sergeants are all buried in the City of London Cemetery.

Fig 32. Sergeant Tucker.
Courtesy of the City of London Police Museum

The Victoria Cross

Britain's highest award for gallantry, the Victoria Cross (Fig 33), dates back one hundred and fifty years, being instituted by Royal Warrant on 29th January 1856, the same year that the City of London Cemetery opened. There are two recipients of the Victoria Cross buried in the City of London Cemetery, John Joseph Sims VC and George Leslie Drewry VC.

John Joseph Sims VC

John Joseph Sims won his VC for his actions in the Crimea War at the Siege of Sebastopol and was one of those present at the very first investiture of the Victoria Cross on Friday 26th June 1857. On this date Queen Victoria presented the new medal to 62 recipients. Sims died in poverty at the age of 46 and was buried in an unmarked 'public grave'. The location of John's Victoria Cross in unknown. The City of London Corporation took the decision in 2003 to place a plaque on the grave of this heroic young man.

Fig 33. The Victoria Cross
Courtesy of the Victoria Cross Website

George Leslie Drewry VC

Our second recipient of the Victoria Cross was awarded to George Leslie Drewry for his actions in the First World War at the Gallipoli landings.

George Leslie Drewry was buried in a private grave and his Victoria Cross is held by the Imperial War Museum in London.

Entertainment Personalities

Herbert Wilcox

Herbert Wilcox was a director and producer of film and was considered to be one of the most important and successful British film-makers from the 1920s up until the 1950s. He was involved in the setting up of Elstree Studios which was known as the British Hollywood and in 1928 he had established the British and Dominions Film Corporation.

Herbert enjoyed a long career in film from the 1920s but his style of film making started to go out of fashion and his last film was *The Heart of a Man* with pop singer Frankie Vaughan in 1959.

Dame Anna Neagle

Marjorie Robertson, who was to take the stage name of Anna Neagle, made her stage début as a dancer in C B Cochran's reviews as early as 1917.

Encouraged by entertainer Jack Buchanan to take a role in the 1931 film *Stand Up and Sing*, Anna's film career blossomed under the direction of her future husband Herbert Wilcox, who was to produce and direct most of her films. Herbert and Anna married in 1943.

Anna stared in a string of popular films up until the mid 1950s when changing tastes saw her box office appeal fade. She and Herbert continued to produce films up until 1959 but they were not successes and lost money. To clear her husband's debts she returned triumphantly to the stage and completed a five-year run in the hit show *Charlie Girl* which ran until 1970.

The British public loved Anna Neagle and she was often voted favourite actress and biggest female box office draw during her time in films. She was awarded a C.B.E. in 1952 and created Dame of the British Empire in 1969.

Fig 34. Herbert Wilcox and Dame Anna Neagle

Memorials of Interest

In the City of London Cemetery there are two memorials that stand out above all of the many others in the 200 acres. They are known as the 'Vigiland', and the 'Piano Lady'. Both of these beautiful memorials commemorate local people.

The Vigiland Memorial

The Vigiland Memorial (Fig 28.) marks the grave of a young man, David John Vigiland RN who died on 20th December 1946 at the age of 20. David was serving overseas in Mombassa at the time of his death and was therefore buried in that country in a cemetery administered by the Imperial War Graves Commission. His distraught father John Vigiland made representations to the Commission to have his son returned to England so that he could be buried in a cemetery locally where he and his wife would be able to visit the grave of their only child.

Permission was refused but John persevered and after a six-year campaign his beloved son was finally brought back to England. David was laid to rest in the City of London Cemetery on 9th December 1952, the date which would have marked his 26th birthday.

The magnificent memorial marking his grave was sculpted in the studios of Pietrasanta, Italy from a 25-ton block of white Sicilian marble, and represents the Descent from the Cross.

The Piano Lady

The second memorial of note is dedicated to the memory of Gladys Spencer, a young music and dance teacher who worked at the Classical Academy of Music and Dancing, in Rixon Road, Manor Park.

Fig 35. Piano Lady Memorial

Gladys was also well known for her local charity work and many were saddened by her death at the early age of 34 years on Easter Monday 1931. Her memorial (Fig 35) features a carving of a grand piano on which a draped figure rests her mourning head.

Churchyard removals
Among the grandest memorials in the cemetery are those raised over the remains removed from demolished City churches. The most impressive is the 1866 memorial, designed by William Haywood in the form of a Gothic Cross, to the dead of St Andrew's and St Sepulchre's Holborn, which

Plate 12. Gardens Way in Memorial Gardens

Plate 13. General Memorial Garden View

Plate 10. Catacomb in winter

Plate 11. City of London Cemetery in the snow

Plate 8. Cemetery Dray Horses

Plate 9. Staff Outing Early 1900's

Plate 7. Burial Chapel (Reserve Chapel)

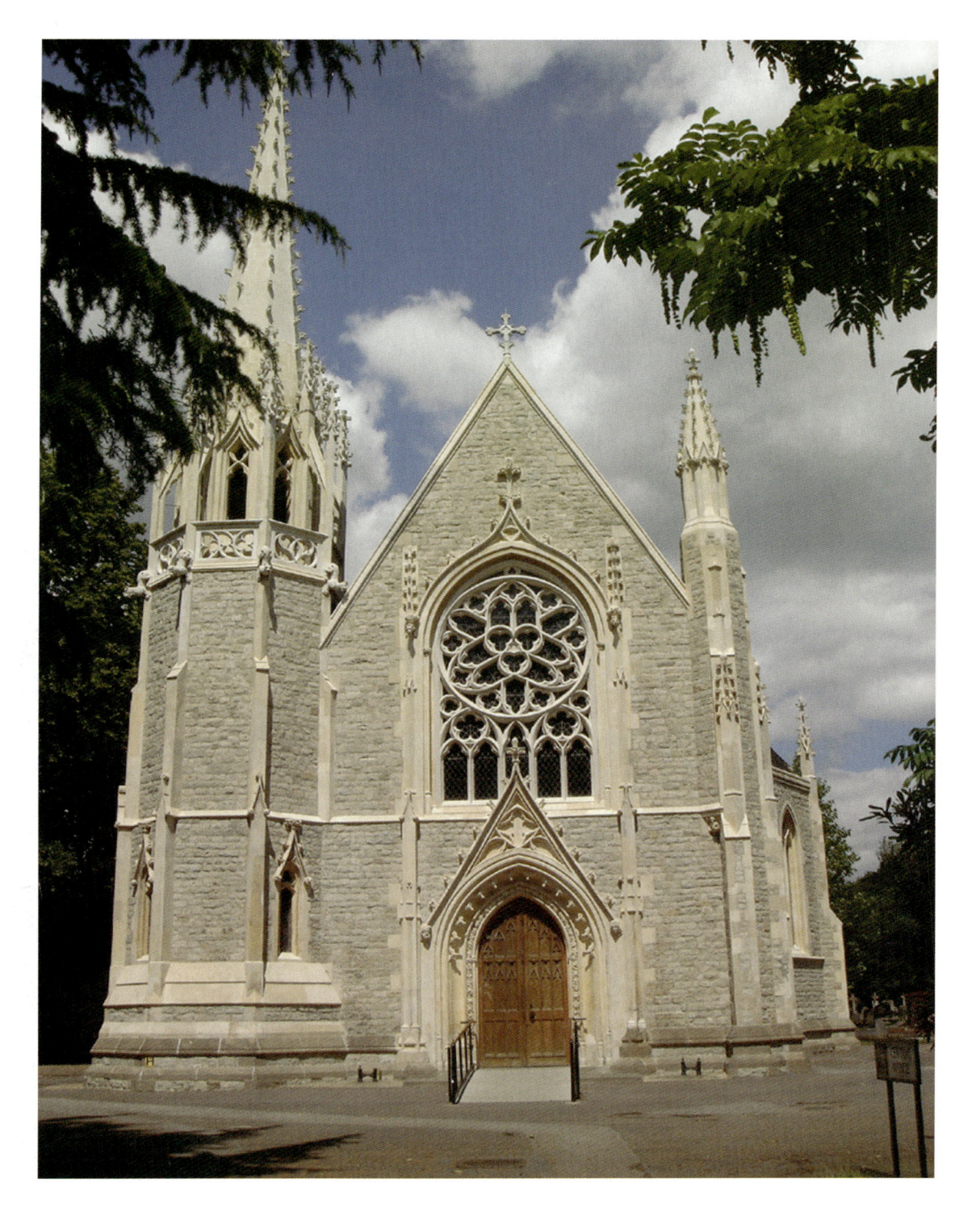

Plate 6. Main Burial Church

Plate 4. View along South Gate Road

Plate 5. Junction of Belfry Road and Anchor Road

Plate 2. Interior of Episcopal Chapel - Main Burial Church

Plate 3. Interior of Dissenters Chapel - Reserve Burial Chapel

Plate 1. *City of London Gates 1913. Courtesy of Funeral Service Journal*

stands in its own railed enclosure. This was located on Central Avenue to be seen along the vista of St Andrew's Avenue from the Chapel. The monument and its garden setting were restored in 2005-06.

Other monuments to the dead of City churchyards are mainly located along Central Avenue and St Dionis Avenue, and include those to All Hallow's Bread Street, which is the second largest, again in a Gothic style; St Helen's Bishopsgate, where the remains of Robert Hooke (1635-1703), the colleague of Christopher Wren known as 'the Leonardo of London,' who designed the Monument to the Great Fire of London, are buried; the eccentric high Gothic memorial to the dead of St Martin's Outwich; the obelisk marking the reinterred remains from the churchyard of St Antholin Watling Street, cleared to make way for the construction of Queen Victoria Street and the great granite block monument marking those of St Mary Woolnoth, removed during the building of the tube station at Bank between 1897 and 1900.